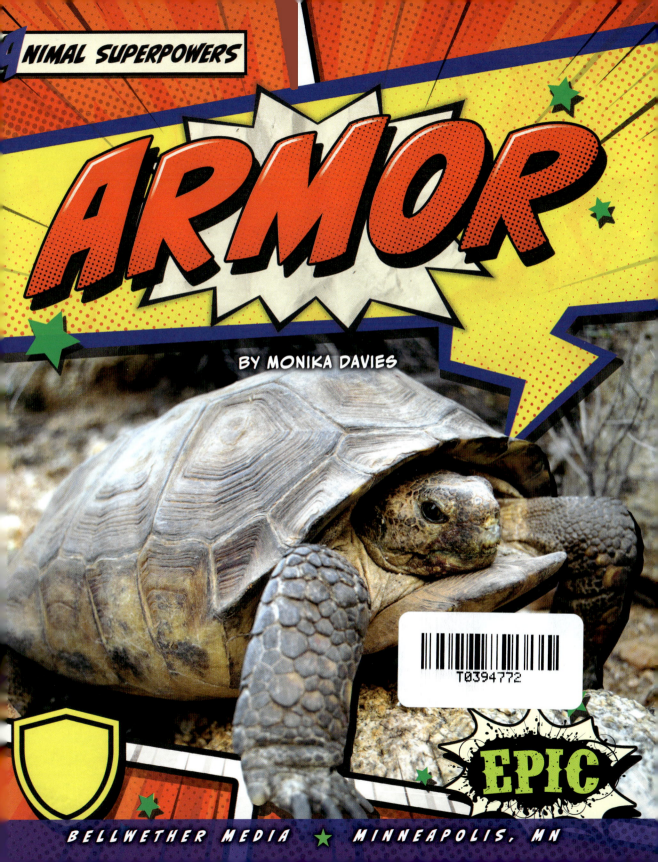

EPIC BOOKS are no ordinary books. They burst with intense action, high-speed heroics, and shadows of the unknown. Are you ready for an Epic adventure?

This edition first published in 2026 by Bellwether Media, Inc.

No part of this publication may be reproduced in whole or in part without written permission of the publisher. For information regarding permission, write to Bellwether Media, Inc., Attention: Permissions Department, 3500 American Blvd W, Suite 150, Bloomington, MN 55431.

Library of Congress Cataloging-in-Publication Data

LC record for Armor available at: https://lccn.loc.gov/2025021807

Text copyright © 2026 by Bellwether Media, Inc. EPIC and associated logos are trademarks and/or registered trademarks of Bellwether Media, Inc. Bellwether Media is a division of FlutterBee Education Group.

Editor: Rachael Barnes   Designer: Gabriel Hilger

Printed in the United States of America, North Mankato, MN.

TABLE OF CONTENTS

SAFE AND SOUND	4
QUILLS THAT STAB	6
SAFE IN THE SHELL	10
DOMED ARMOR	14
SPIKED SCALES	18
GLOSSARY	22
TO LEARN MORE	23
INDEX	24

SAFE AND SOUND

Humans wear thick vests and helmets as armor. But many animals grow their own armor!

Some animal armor is thick. Other armor is sharp. Armor **protects** animals from harm.

QUILLS THAT STAB

Porcupines may look soft. But they have an armor of hard, sharp **quills**. There are around 30,000 quills on a porcupine's body.

Quills can **pierce** an enemy's skin. Their sharp edges make them hard to remove!

QUILL

NORTH AMERICAN PORCUPINE

CLASS: MAMMAL

LIFE SPAN: UP TO 18 YEARS

STATUS IN THE WILD

| LEAST CONCERN | NEAR THREATENED | VULNERABLE | ENDANGERED | CRITICALLY ENDANGERED | EXTINCT IN THE WILD | EXTINCT |

RANGE

7

HOLLOW HAIR
Porcupine quills are hollow inside!

Porcupines run from **predators**. Sometimes they get trapped. They turn their back and raise their sharp quills. They are ready for an attack.

QUILLS IN ACTION!

Porcupines swing their tails. Their quills stab their enemy. Porcupines stay safe!

SAFE IN THE SHELL

SHELL

When it is hot outside, desert tortoises live in **burrows**. They come out in cooler weather to eat and drink.

Their shells keep them safe outside!

MOJAVE DESERT TORTOISE

CLASS: REPTILE

LIFE SPAN: UP TO 80 YEARS

STATUS IN THE WILD

| LEAST CONCERN | NEAR THREATENED | VULNERABLE | ENDANGERED | CRITICALLY ENDANGERED | EXTINCT IN THE WILD | EXTINCT |

RANGE

11

Desert tortoise shells are made mostly of strong bone. Shells harden as they age.

DOMED ARMOR

SHELL

TAIL

Horseshoe crabs crawl across the sand. Their long tails slide behind them.

These **arthropods** are known for their large, **domed** shells. Horseshoe crabs live in their armor!

AMERICAN HORSESHOE CRAB

CLASS: ARTHROPOD

LIFE SPAN: AROUND 20 YEARS

STATUS IN THE WILD

| LEAST CONCERN | NEAR THREATENED | VULNERABLE | ENDANGERED | CRITICALLY ENDANGERED | EXTINCT IN THE WILD | EXTINCT |

RANGE

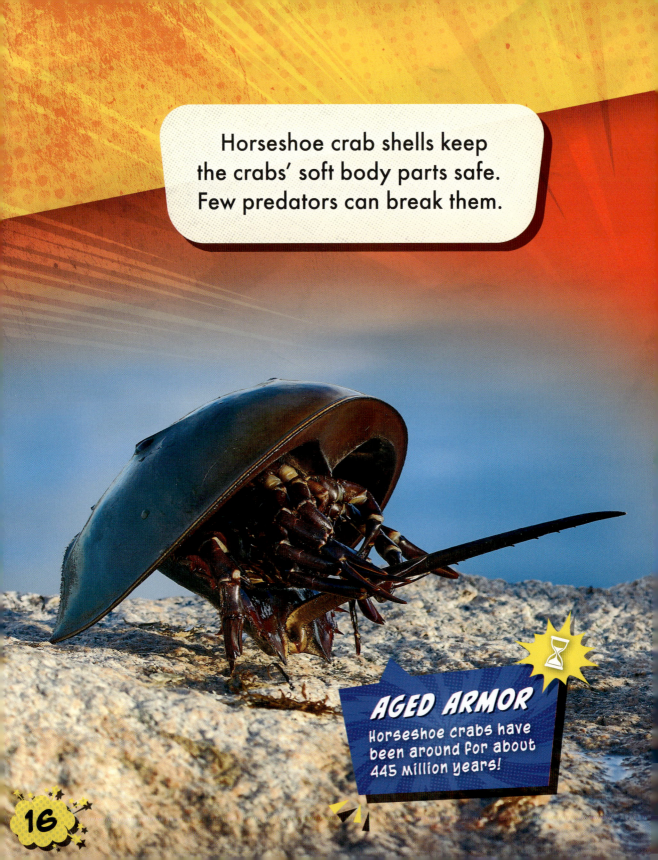

Horseshoe crab shells keep the crabs' soft body parts safe. Few predators can break them.

AGED ARMOR
Horseshoe crabs have been around for about 445 million years!

EMPTY SHELL

Horseshoe crabs **shed** their shells as they grow. During its life, one crab can have up to 17 shells!

SPIKED SCALES

SCALES

Armadillo lizards look like tiny dragons. Sharp **scales** run along their backs. The scales act as armor!

These lizards live in **shrublands** and rocky areas of South Africa. They hide in holes between rocks.

Armadillo Girdled Lizard

CLASS: REPTILE

LIFE SPAN: 20 TO 25 YEARS

Status in the Wild

| Least Concern | Near Threatened | Vulnerable | Endangered | Critically Endangered | Extinct in the Wild | Extinct |

▼ (Near Threatened)

RANGE

These lizards have soft bellies. If they get scared, they curl into a spiky ball. The lizards bite their tail. This keeps their bellies hidden.

SCALES IN ACTION!

20

GLOSSARY

arthropods—animals with segmented bodies and no backbone; most arthropods have exoskeletons that they shed from time to time.

burrows—holes or tunnels in the ground used as animals' homes

domed—rounded on top with a circular base

pierce—to make a hole in or through

predators—animals that hunt other animals for food

protects—keeps something or someone safe

quills—sharp, hollow spines on a porcupine

scales—small plates that cover and protect an animal's body

shed—to lose something on the body such as fur or skin

shrublands—dry lands that have mostly low plants and few trees

TO LEARN MORE

AT THE LIBRARY

Perish, Patrick. *Desert Tortoises*. Minneapolis, Minn.: Bellwether Media, 2021.

Scheffer, Janie. *Porcupines*. Minneapolis, Minn.: Bellwether Media, 2026.

Somaweera, Ruchira. *The Ultimate Book of Reptiles: Your Guide to the Secret Lives of These Scaly, Slithery, and Spectacular Creatures.* Washington, D.C.: National Geographic, 2023.

ON THE WEB

FACTSURFER

Factsurfer.com gives you a safe, fun way to find more information.

1. Go to www.factsurfer.com.

2. Enter "armor" into the search box and click 🔍.

3. Select your book cover to see a list of related content.

INDEX

age, 12, 16
American horseshoe crab, 15
armadillo girdled lizard, 19
armadillo lizards, 18, 19, 20, 21
arthropods, 15
attack, 8
backs, 18
bellies, 20
body, 6, 16
burrows, 10
desert tortoises, 10, 11, 12, 13
hide, 13, 19, 20
horseshoe crabs, 14, 15, 16, 17
Mojave desert tortoise, 11
name, 21

North American porcupine, 7
porcupines, 6, 7, 8, 9
predators, 7, 8, 9, 13, 16
protects, 4
quills, 6, 7, 8, 9
quills in action, 9
range, 7, 11, 15, 19
scales, 18
scales in action, 20
shed, 17
shells, 10, 11, 12, 13, 14, 15, 16, 17
shrublands, 19
South Africa, 19
tails, 9, 14, 20
turtle, 13
weather, 10

The images in this book are reproduced through the courtesy of: Tim Fitzharris/ Minden, front cover; Tomaz, p. 3; Natural History Archive/ Alamy Stock Photo, p. 4; Michael Nicolai, pp. 5, 18; hkuchera, p. 6; Custom Life Science Images/ Alamy Stock Photo, p. 7 (quill); Nick Fox, p. 7 (class: mammal); Jens, pp. 8-9; imageBROKER.com/ Alamy Stock Photo, p. 9 (quills down); Konrad Wothe/ Minden, p. 9 (quills up); Gchapel, p. 10; Irina K., p. 11 (inset); William Mullins/ Alamy Stock Photo, p. 11 (class: reptile); PixyNL, p. 12; Michael Sayles/ Alamy Stock Photo, p. 13; Takis, p. 14; slowmotiongli, p. 15 (inset); viktor2013, p. 15 (class: arthropod); Weblogiq, p. 16; Jaclyn Vernace, p. 17 (empty shell); driftlessstudio, p. 17; Eric Isselee, p. 18 (scales); piemags/ nature/ Alamy Stock Photo, p. 19 (inset); Lauren Suryanata, p. 19 (class: reptile); Kevin Murray/ Wikipedia, p. 20 (uncurled spikes); bdfhbdx/ Wikipedia, p. 20 (curled spikes); Thorsten Spoerlein, p. 21; Eric Isselée, p. 22.